Volume 99 of the Yale Series of Younger Poets

Crush

20TH ANNIVERSARY EDITION

RICHARD SIKEN

WITH A NEW AFTERWORD BY THE AUTHOR

FOREWORD BY LOUISE GLÜCK

INTRODUCTION BY DANA LEVIN

Yale University Press/New Haven & London

2oth Anniversary Edition, 2025

Published with assistance from a grant to honor James Merrill.

Originally published in 2005 by Yale University Press.

Designed by Mary Valencia.
Set in Fournier type by Integrated Publishing Solutions.
Printed in the United States of America.

The Library of Congress has cataloged the original edition as follows:
Siken, Richard, 1967–
    Crush / Richard Siken ; foreword by Louise Glück.
    p. cm. — (The Yale series of younger poets ; v. 99)
ISBN 0-300-10721-8 (cloth : alk. paper)
ISBN 0-300-10789-7 (pbk. : alk. paper)
    I. Title. II. Series.
PS3619.I48C78 2005
811′.6—dc22   2004054184

ISBN 978-0-300-27857-6 (hardcover:alk.paper)
Library of Congress Control Number: 2024943260

A catalogue record for this book is available from the British Library.

This paper meets the requirements of ANSI/NISO Z39.48-1992
(Permanence of Paper).

10 9 8 7 6 5 4 3 2 1

Contents

Introduction

One day, more than twenty years ago, I came home from work and found a large heavy box under the spindly elm outside my studio apartment, where the mail carrier had unceremoniously dropped it. I lugged it in, sat on the floor, and opened it: inside, stacks of manuscripts, each one submitted in hopes of winning the Yale Younger Poets Prize. Established in 1918, the Yale Series of Younger Poets prize is the oldest and arguably most prestigious of the publication prizes open solely to debut poets in the United States. For a long stretch of its history, it was the only prize of its kind.

I was one of several poets who had been tasked with screening submissions for Louise Glück, who was then the contest judge. After dinner, I lifted the submissions out of the box, piled them on the floor, and started my survey. I felt Glück's exacting eye on each manuscript I scanned, her instructions firm: "Send it on if it has a pulse."

Finally, after skimming many, I encountered a manuscript that felt blazingly alive. What I remember most is how lines vibrated, raw and bristly, before I even closely read the poems in which they appeared. In these lines I could feel hints of that pulse Glück was looking for: "These, our bodies, possessed by light," in a poem called "Scheherazade"; "I'll be your / slaughterhouse, your killing floor, your morgue" in a poem called "Wishbone." And in "Litany in Which Certain Things Are Crossed Out," these lines, which stopped me in my tracks:

> Dear So-and-So, I'm sorry I couldn't come to your party.
> Dear So-and-So, I'm sorry I came to your party
>   and seduced you
> and left you bruised and ruined, you poor sad thing.

The brash tone! The sorry-not-sorry. The *confidence*. I started to read the poems closely. They were inviting and hostile, intimate and defensive, urgent and afraid and yearning. The speaker seemed both incredibly candid and deeply unreliable. The poems were often heartbreaking, figuratively and literally—I was never sure if the speaker would get out of loving alive (and neither was the speaker). There was nothing else like it in that heavy box I had hoisted through my door.

I knew I had found a manuscript that moved beyond the merely accomplished—an attribute that can be applied to so many manuscripts vying for attention. What separates the extraordinary from the accomplished and makes the accomplished feel *mere?* A living hand, warm and capable—here, a hand that seemed capable of murder, of self-immolation: *"Sorry / about the blood in your mouth. I wish it was mine"* ("Little Beast").

The manuscript I'd found became the book *Crush,* by Richard Siken. And over its twenty years of existence, it has thrilled and moved thousands of readers. Since it was published in 2005, it has sold well over 100,000 copies—a head-spinning count for a debut book of poetry. It has also sold widely in foreign translation: in Arabic, Chinese, Czech, Danish, Greek, Spanish, and Swedish. Its persistent popularity is stunning: according to Nielsen BookScan, for the entirety of *Crush*'s published life, not a week has gone by without someone, somewhere, buying a copy.

One primary factor accounting for its longevity is that *Crush* has become a crucial text for many gay and queer readers. I reached out to some of those readers, Siken's peers, to find out how the book had affected them when they first read it. Brian Teare, author of the award-winning *Doomstead Days,* told me about his time on the editorial staff of *Indiana Review* in the late 1990s, when the journal featured a lot of the poems that would end up in *Crush:* "We were ALL obsessed with Siken's work! But for me, a gay poet coming of age during the HIV/AIDS era, when comparatively few young gay poets were publishing books, Siken's work was revelatory—it conveyed what Glück would later call 'panic' that to my mind wasn't only specific to the book's speaker. It was generational and American, the felt reality of being young and gay in the US during HIV/AIDS and its attendant conservative cultural backlash."

Eduardo C. Corral, 2011 winner of the Yale Younger Poets Prize for *Slow Lightning,* remembered reading *Crush* in a Borders bookstore: "I'd graduated from Iowa in 2001 and was still trying to figure out the languages spiraling in my mind. I was anxious, impatient. *Crush* encouraged me to keep obsessing over language, to keep unpacking language. It became a book I leaned into, pushed against, as I worked on my first book." Ocean Vuong, author of 2016's *Night Sky with Exit Wounds,* which has had its own extraordinary life as a debut book of poetry, wrote: "The immense wingspan of influence that *Crush* has on 21st-century American poetry cannot be overstated. Not only does Siken center Queer yearning, he fills those poems with the detritus of life—the cacti, taco stands, twenty-four-hour supermarkets, interstates, boots, and shag rugs—a project begun by William Carlos Williams, and here made palpable, enriched and enlarged, to a whole new generation." And Randall Mann, author of *Deal: New and Selected Poems*, brought his first impressions of *Crush* to vivid life, recalling: "Well, there was the Cooper blurb, which all us queers gagged on, the word *complicit;* the (presumably) bloody, queasy thumbprint on the cover; the word *tyrant* Louise Glück used to describe the body in the introduction. And by the time I got to the end of the second poem, 'Dirty Valentine'—"The world is no longer mysterious"—I was heartbroken, and hooked. I'm still. I found Siken in the ether, and wrote to him about the book; his reply closed, naturally, as follows: 'Do you have a nemesis? Do you want to be a superhero? I think we should fight.'"

Many poetry readers may not know this, but there's a secret to *Crush*'s enduring popularity too; it rests not in the hands of the literati or the professors, but in the rough and Tumblr realms of the internet. Google "Siken" and "Supernatural" and "Sherlock" and "fanfic" and you will find entry into a whole world of people who quote Siken, who meme Siken lines, who insist *Crush* was written for and about characters on television shows, no matter how often Siken has tried to correct them. Petrana Radulovic, a writer for *Polygon,* an entertainment website covering video games and popular culture, wrote in 2023, "Siken's poetry has long been a fundamental part of the fandom experience, particularly for those who are extremely online. Fans across tons of different TV shows, movies, and games—particularly those with big slash (male-male pairings) ships—have added lines from his poetry as captions on their fanart for years, superimposed it on yearning gif edits, or even titled their own fanfiction with it."

Siken has embraced the fans who have found his work this way, saying in his own 2015 Tumblr post on the phenomenon: "Remix culture. Metamodernism. Fan fiction, screen caps, memes. That's where our heads are right now . . . If we mention Mnemosyne, it's labeled High Art. If we mention *Sherlock* (the television show), it's labeled Low Art. But it's the same thing. These references, these allusions, are landmarks. We use them to plant flags and share meaning."

Two years ago, when Siken returned to X (formerly Twitter) after much time away, his fans followed. He found himself an inadvertent advice columnist, inundated daily with questions sincere, provocative, and ridiculous. He tries to respond as much as he can. When asked about this in a 2023 interview for *The*

Adroit Journal, Siken said, "I came out a few months before AIDS hit hard. The generation above me was decimated. The potential role models and guides I might have had were wiped out. The people who were going to protect me were eliminated . . . I try to be as attentive and careful as I can, because we're still recovering from the loss. Sometimes I get sloppy or frustrated or glib, but I try to be available and tender." At times, fans get too close, looking to Siken for aid better offered by a trained counselor; sometimes the exchanges with fans are fun and energizing: "The thing I like the most is when I get clipped or shouldered in just the right way and I surprise myself . . . Someone said, 'I'd go to war for Richard Siken,' and for whatever reason, I replied, 'We are not going to war, we are going to the club. Put on your good shoes.' I think that's my favorite exchange so far."

As much as *Crush* has met cultural need and trend over the last twenty years, its central concern is an eternal one: desire—its intoxications and compulsions, its difficulty and terror. Whether expressed via high art or low, in poetry or in a meme, desire is one of art's perennial subjects because it's a central human experience: it makes us suffer; it brings us joy; it changes us; it crushes us. *Crush* debuted at a time "when being gay was de facto conflated with personal and collective traumas," Teare said in his email to me. "The hyper-aroused, highly cinematic aesthetic of Siken's poems reflected that perfectly—and in important ways that could also pass for the ordinary arousals and melodramas of young love."

For readers who are encountering *Crush* for the first time or revisiting it after years away, I close with something Siken said in a 2014 interview with *Black Warrior Review,* when asked what he hoped to find in the poems he read: "I want to be overthrown or undone, stunned by something I'd never heard before or I'd ever thought of . . . I want it to spin against the way it drives. I want friction and tension . . . Just get me there." *Crush* got me there all those years ago in my little apartment, as I settled in and read the manuscript from start to finish. I join a legion of fans celebrating the reissue of this essential, electrifying book.

Dana Levin

Foreword

This is a book about panic. The word is never mentioned. Nor is the condition analyzed or described—the speaker is never outside it long enough to differentiate panic from other states. In the world of *Crush*, panic is a synonym for being: in its delays, in its swerving and rushing syntax, its frantic lists and questions, it fends off time and loss. Its opposite is oblivion: not the tranquil oblivion of sleep but the threatening oblivions of sex and death. The poems' power derives from obsession, but Richard Siken's manner is sheer manic improv, with the poet in all the roles: he is the animal trapped in the headlights, paralyzed; he is also the speeding vehicle, the car that doesn't stop, the mechanism of flight. The book is all high beams: reeling, savage, headlong, insatiable:

> . . . Names called out across the water,
> names I called you behind your back,
> sour and delicious, secret and unrepeatable,
> the names of flowers that open only once,
> shouted from balconies, shouted from rooftops,
> or muffled by pillows, or whispered in sleep,
> or caught in the throat like a lump of meat.
> I try, I do. I try and try. A happy ending?
> Sure enough—*Hello darling, welcome home.*

The poem can't stop:

> . . . Names of heat and names of light,
> names of collision in the dark, on the side of the
> bus, in the bark of the tree, in ballpoint pen
> on jeans and hands and the backs of matchbooks
> that then get lost. Names like pain cries, names
> like tombstones, names forgotten and reinvented,
> names forbidden or overused. . . .
> > "Saying Your Names"

Or, in "Wishbone":

> I'm bleeding, I'm not just making conversation.
> There's smashed glass glittering everywhere like stars. It's a Western,
> Henry. It's a downright shoot-em-up. We've made a graveyard
>   out of the bone white afternoon.

and later:

> Even when you're standing up
> you look like you're lying down, but will you let me kiss your neck, baby?
> Do I have to tie your arms down? Do I have to stick my tongue in your
>   mouth like the hand of a thief,
> like a burglary, . . .

The poems' desperate garrulousness delays catastrophe. Accumulation and reiteration avert some impact, some deadly connection. This is also the way one would address an absence, allowing no pause for the silence that would constitute response.

That Siken turns life into art seems, in these poems, psychological imperative rather than literary ploy: the poems substitute the repeating cycles of ritual for linear progressive time—in *Crush*, the bullet enters the body and then returns to the gun. Cameras are everywhere, and tapes, the means by which an instant can be replayed over and over, manipulated. The poems' tense playbacks and freeze frames —their strategies of control—delineate chilling certainties and immutabilities. Which means, of course, the poems are driven by what they deny; their ferocity attests to the depth of their terror, their resourcefulness to the intractability of the enemy's presence. Everything is a trick, the poems say, everything is art, technology—everything, that is, can still change. This is Siken's way of saying the reverse: in these poems, everything is harrowing and absolute and deadly real:

> It was night for many miles and then the real stars in the purple sky,
>   like little boats rowed out too far,
> begin to disappear.
>   And there, in the distance, not the promised land,
>   but a Holiday Inn,
> with bougainvillea growing through the chain link by the pool.
>   The door swung wide: twin beds, twin lamps, twin plastic cups
> wrapped up in cellophane

and he says *No Henry, let's not do this.*
Can you see the plot like dotted lines across the room?
Here is the sink to wash away the blood,
here's the whiskey, the ripped-up shirt. Here is the tile of the bathroom
floor, the disk of the drain
punched through with holes.
Here is the boy like a sack of meat, here are the engines, the little room
that is not a room,
the Henry that is not a Henry, the Henry with a needle and thread,
hovering over the hollow boy passed out
on the universal bedspread.

Time passes:

The bell rings, the dog growls,
and then the wind picking up, and the light falling,
and the window closing tight against the dirty rain.

And later:

He puts his hands all over you to keep you in the room.
It's night. It's noon. He's driving. It's happening
all over again.

. . . .

I've been in your body, baby, and it was paradise.
I've been in your body and it was a carnival ride.
"The Dislocated Room"

If panic is his groundnote, Siken's obsessive focus is a tyrant, the body. His title, *Crush,* suggests as much. In the dictionary, among the word's many meanings, "to press between opposing bodies so as to break or injure; to oppress; to break, pound or grind." Or, as a noun, "extreme pressure." Out of this cauldron of destruction, its informal meaning: infatuation, the sweet fixation of girl on boy. In Siken, boy on boy. In its fusion of the erotic and the life-threatening, the inescapable, *Crush* suggests *The Story of O,* although bondage here is less literal. Sometimes the poems that most sharply delineate this obsession work from the moment outward and backward, in waves; sometimes we get eerie flashbacks, succinct, comprehensive, premonitory, as in the first section of "A Primer for the Small Weird Loves," thirteen lines that predict and summarize a life:

> The blond boy in the red trunks is holding your head underwater
> because he is trying to kill you,
> and you deserve it, you do, and you know this,
> and you are ready to die in this swimming pool
> because you wanted to touch his hands and lips and this means
> your life is over anyway.
> You're in the eighth grade. You know these things.
> You know how to ride a dirt bike, and you know how to do
> long division,
> and you know that a boy who likes boys is a dead boy, unless
> he keeps his mouth shut, which is what you
> didn't do,
> because you are weak and hollow and it doesn't matter anymore.

For a book like this to work, it cannot deviate from obsession (lest its urgency, in being occasional, seem unconvincing). Books of this kind dream big; they trust not only what drives them but the importance of what drives them. When they work, as Plath's *Ariel* works, they are unforgettable; they restore to poetry that sense of crucial moment and crucial utterance which may indeed be the great genius of the form. But the problems of such undertakings are immense; Plath's thousand imitators cannot sustain her intensity or her resourcefulness. The risk of obsessive material is that it may get boring, repetitious, predictable, shrill. And the triumph of *Crush* is that it writhes and blazes while at the same time holding the reader utterly: "sustaining interest" seems far too mild a term for this effect. What holds is sheer art, despite the apparent abandon. Siken has a brilliant sense of juxtaposition, a wily self-consciousness, an impeccable sense of timing. He can slip into his hurtling unstoppable sentences and fragments moments of viciously catty wit, passages of epigrammatic virtuosity:

> Someone once told me that explaining is an admission of failure.
> I'm sure you remember, I was on the phone with you, sweetheart.
> "Little Beast"

> . . . This is where the evening
> splits in half, Henry, love or death. Grab an end, pull hard,
> and make a wish.
>
> "Wishbone"

Some of these have a plangency and luster we haven't expected:

> Every story has its chapter in the desert, the long slide from kingdom
> to kingdom through the wilderness,
> where you learn things, where you're left to your own devices.
>
> "Driving, Not Washing"

Inevitability and closure haunt these poems; the deferred, the fated—impending loss and deserved punishment—suffuse every line. The poems draw a feverish energy from what they don't really believe: even as the speaker lives his strategies, he doesn't believe in his own escape. Not every poem operates this way. Siken occasionally locates a poem in loss as enacted, not implicit, event. These are among his most beautiful poems, their capitulations heartbreaking in the context of prolonged animal struggle against acknowledgment. One begins the book, positioning the reader as complicitous:

> Tell me about the dream where we pull the bodies out of the lake
> and dress them in warm clothes again.
> How it was late, and no one could sleep, the horses running
> until they forget that they are horses.
> It's not like a tree where the roots have to end somewhere,
> it's more like a song on a policeman's radio,
> how we rolled up the carpet so we could dance, and the days
> were bright red, and every time we kissed there was another apple
> to slice into pieces.
> Look at the light through the windowpane. That means it's noon, that means
> we're inconsolable.
> Tell me how all this, and love too, will ruin us.
> These, our bodies, possessed by light.
> Tell me we'll never get used to it.
>
> "Scheherazade"

Tell me, the poet says, the lie I need to feel safe, and tell me in your own voice, so I believe you. One more tale to stay alive.

It is difficult, given the length of Siken's characteristic poems, to convey in an introduction a sense of their cumulative, driving, apocalyptic power, their purgatorial recklessness. In other ways, this introduction has been difficult; because of the poems' interconnectedness, the temptation has been to quote everything. Such difficulty is, in itself, praise of the work.

We live in a period of great polarities: in art, in public policy, in morality. In poetry, art seems, at one extreme, rhymed good manners, and at the other, chaos. The great task has been to infuse clarity with the passionate ferment of the inchoate, the chaotic.

Siken takes to heart this exhortation. *Crush* is the best example I can presently give of profound wildness that is also completely intelligible. By Higginson's report, Emily Dickinson famously remarked, "If I read a book and it makes my whole body so cold no fire can warm me, I know that it is poetry. If I feel physically as if the top of my head were taken off, I know that it is poetry. These are the only ways I know it. Is there any other way?"

She should, in that remark, have shamed forever the facile, the decorative, the easily consoling, the tame. She names, after all, responses that suggest violent transformation, the overturning of complacency by peril.

In practice, this has meant that poets quote Dickinson and proceed to write poems from which will and caution and hunger to accommodate present taste have drained all authenticity and unnerving originality. Richard Siken, with the best poets of his impressive generation, has chosen to take Dickinson at her word. I had her reaction.

Louise Glück

Acknowledgments

Grateful acknowledgment is made to the editors of the publications in which the following poems, some in alternate versions, first appeared:

Chelsea: "Boot Theory"

Conjunctions: "You Are Jeff"

Eoagh: "Road Music"

Forklift, Ohio: "Saying Your Names"

Indiana Review: "Scheherazade," "Litany in Which Certain Things Are Crossed Out," "A Primer for the Small Weird Loves," "Straw House, Straw Dog," "The Dislocated Room," "Meanwhile"

Iowa Review: "The Torn-Up Road," "I Had a Dream About You"

Jackleg: "Visible World"

Lit: "Driving, Not Washing"

Many Mountains Moving: "Wishbone"

Sonora Review: "Dirty Valentine"

The Best American Poetry 2000: "The Dislocated Room"

The Pushcart Prize XXV: Best of Small Presses: "A Primer for the Small Weird Loves"

Sections of "Little Beast" were published under this and other titles in *Iowa Review* and *The James White Review*

I

Scheherazade

Tell me about the dream where we pull the bodies out of the lake
                                        and dress them in warm clothes again.
     How it was late, and no one could sleep, the horses running
until they forget that they are horses.
          It's not like a tree where the roots have to end somewhere,
          it's more like a song on a policeman's radio,
               how we rolled up the carpet so we could dance, and the days
were bright red, and every time we kissed there was another apple
                                             to slice into pieces.
Look at the light through the windowpane. That means it's noon, that means
     we're inconsolable.
                    Tell me how all this, and love too, will ruin us.
These, our bodies, possessed by light.
                         Tell me we'll never get used to it.

Dirty Valentine

There are so many things I'm not allowed to tell you.
I touch myself, I dream.
Wearing your clothes or standing in the shower for over an hour, pretending
that this skin is your skin, these hands your hands,
these shins, these soapy flanks.
The musicians start the overture while I hide behind the microphone,
trying to match the dubbing
to the big lips shining down from the screen.
We're filming the movie called *Planet of Love*—
there's sex of course, and ballroom dancing,
fancy clothes and waterlilies in the pond, and half the night you're
a dependable chap, mounting the stairs in lamplight to the bath, but then
the too white teeth all night,
all over the American sky, too much to bear, this constant fingering,
your hands a river gesture, the birds in flight, the birds still singing
outside the greasy window, in the trees.
There's a part in the movie
where you can see right through the acting,
where you can tell that I'm about to burst into tears,
right before I burst into tears
and flee to the slimy moonlit riverbed
canopied with devastated clouds.
We're shooting the scene where I swallow your heart and you make me
spit it up again. I swallow your heart and it crawls
right out of my mouth.
You swallow my heart and flee, but I want it back now, baby. I want it back.
Lying on the sofa with my eyes closed, I didn't want to see it this way,
everything eating everything in the end.
We know how the light works,
we know where the sound is coming from.
Verse. Chorus. Verse.
I'm sorry. We know how it works. The world is no longer mysterious.

Little Beast

1

An all-night barbeque. A dance on the courthouse lawn.
        The radio aches a little tune that tells the story of what the night
is thinking. It's thinking of love.
                        It's thinking of stabbing us to death
and leaving our bodies in a dumpster.
        That's a nice touch, stains in the night, whiskey and kisses for everyone.

Tonight, by the freeway, a man eating fruit pie with a buckknife
        carves the likeness of his lover's face into the motel wall. I like him
and I want to be like him, my hands no longer an afterthought.

2

Someone once told me that explaining is an admission of failure.
        I'm sure you remember, I was on the phone with you, sweetheart.

3

History repeats itself. Somebody says this.
                History throws its shadow over the beginning, over the desktop,
over the sock drawer with its socks, its hidden letters.
                                History is a little man in a brown suit
        trying to define a room he is outside of.
I know history. There are many names in history
                                but none of them are ours.

4

He had green eyes,
                so I wanted to sleep with him—

green eyes flecked with yellow, dried leaves on the surface of a pool—
You could drown in those eyes, I said.
                                        The fact of his pulse,
the way he pulled his body in, out of shyness or shame or a desire
        not to disturb the air around him.
Everyone could see the way his muscles worked,
                        the way we look like animals,
                                        his skin barely keeping him inside.

        I wanted to take him home
and rough him up and get my hands inside him, drive my body into his
        like a crash test car.
                        I wanted to be wanted and he was
very beautiful, kissed with his eyes closed, and only felt good while moving.
        You could drown in those eyes, I said,
                                        so it's summer, so it's suicide,
so we're helpless in sleep and struggling at the bottom of the pool.

        5

It wasn't until we were well past the middle of it
        that we realized
the old dull pain, whose stitched wrists and clammy fingers,
                                        far from being subverted,
had only slipped underneath us, freshly scrubbed.
                        Mirrors and shop windows returned our faces to us,
        replete with the tight lips and the eyes that remained eyes
                        and not the doorways we had hoped for.
His wounds healed, the skin a bit thicker than before,
        scars like train tracks on his arms and on his body underneath his shirt.

        6

We still groped for each other on the backstairs or in parked cars
                                as the roads around us
grew glossy with ice and our breath softened the view through a glass

already laced with frost,
but more frequently I was finding myself sleepless, and he was running out of
lullabies.
But damn if there isn't anything sexier
than a slender boy with a handgun,
a fast car, a bottle of pills.

7

What would you like? I'd like my money's worth.
Try explaining a life bundled with episodes of this—
swallowing mud, swallowing glass, the smell of blood
on the first four knuckles.
We pull our boots on with both hands
but we can't punch ourselves awake and all I can do
is stand on the curb and say *Sorry*
about the blood in your mouth. I wish it was mine.

I couldn't get the boy to kill me, but I wore his jacket for the longest time.

Seaside Improvisation

I take off my hands and I give them to you but you don't
                              want them, so I take them back
    and put them on the wrong way, the wrong wrists. The yard is dark,
the tomatoes are next to the whitewashed wall,
                    the book on the table is about Spain,
                                    the windows are painted shut.
Tonight you're thinking of cities under crowns
            of snow and I stare at you like I'm looking through a window,
                                    counting birds.
                    You wanted happiness, I can't blame you for that,
and maybe a mouth sounds idiotic when it blathers on about joy
    but tell me
you love this, tell me you're not miserable.
                        You do the math, you expect the trouble.
        The seaside town. The electric fence.
Draw a circle with a piece of chalk. Imagine standing in a constant cone
            of light. Imagine surrender. Imagine being useless.
A stone on the path means the tea's not ready,
    a stone in the hand means somebody's angry, the stone inside you still
hasn't hit bottom.

The Torn-Up Road

1

There is no way to make this story interesting.

A pause, a road, the taste of gravel in the mouth. The rocks dig into my skin
   like arrowheads.
And then the sense of being smothered underneath a sack of lentils
         or potatoes, or of a boat at night slamming into the dock again
                     without navigation, without consideration,
heedless of the planks of wood that are the dock,
                           that make up the berth itself.

2

   I want to tell you this story without having to confess anything,
without having to say that I ran out into the street to prove something,
                           that he didn't love me,
   that I wanted to be thrown over, possessed.
               I want to tell you this story without having to be in it:
   Max in the wrong clothes. Max at the party, drunk again.
Max in the kitchen, in refrigerator light, his hands around the neck of a beer.
               Tell me we're dead and I'll love you even more.
I'm surprised that I say it with feeling.
   There's a thing in my stomach about this. A simple thing. The last rung.

3

Can you see them there, by the side of the road,
                           not moving, not wrestling,
making a circle out of the space between the circles? Can you see them
   pressed into the gravel, pressed into the dirt, pressing against each other
in an effort to make the minutes stop—

headlights shining in all directions, night spilling over them like
gasoline in all directions, and the dark blue over everything, and them
                                        holding their breath—

4

I want to tell you this story without having to say that I ran out into the street
                            to prove something, that he chased after me
        and threw me into the gravel.
And he knew it wasn't going to be okay, and he told me
                                        it wasn't going to be okay.
And he wouldn't kiss me, but he covered my body with his body
        and held me down until I promised not to run back out into the street again.

But the minutes don't stop. The prayer of going nowhere
                                        going nowhere.

5

His shoulder blots out the stars but the minutes don't stop. He covers my body
        with his body but the minutes
don't stop. The smell of him mixed with creosote, exhaust—
                        There, on the ground, slipping through the minutes,
trying to notch them. Like taking the same picture over and over, the spaces
    in between sealed up—
Knocked hard enough to make the record skip
                        and change its music, setting the melody on its
forward course again, circling and circling the center hole in the flat black disk.
        And words, little words,
words too small for any hope or promise, not really soothing
                                        but soothing nonetheless.

Litany in Which Certain Things Are Crossed Out

Every morning the maple leaves.
                    Every morning another chapter where the hero shifts
         from one foot to the other. Every morning the same big
and little words all spelling out desire, all spelling out
                              You will be alone always and then you will die.
So maybe I wanted to give you something more than a catalog
         of non-definitive acts,
something other than the desperation.
                    Dear So-and-So, I'm sorry I couldn't come to your party.
Dear So-and-So, I'm sorry I came to your party
         and seduced you
and left you bruised and ruined, you poor sad thing.
                              You want a better story. Who wouldn't?
A forest, then. Beautiful trees. And a lady singing
         Love on the water, love underwater, love, love and so on.
What a sweet lady. Sing lady, sing! Of course, she wakes the dragon.
         Love always wakes the dragon and suddenly
                              flames everywhere.
I can tell already you think I'm the dragon,
         that would be so like me, but I'm not. I'm not the dragon.
I'm not the princess either.
                    Who am I? I'm just a writer. I write things down.
I walk through your dreams and invent the future. Sure,
         I sink the boat of love, but that comes later. And yes, I swallow
     glass, but that comes later.
                    And the part where I push you
flush against the wall and every part of your body rubs against the bricks,
         shut up
I'm getting to it.
                    For a while I thought I was the dragon.
I guess I can tell you that now. And, for a while, I thought I was
                              the princess,

11

cotton candy pink, sitting there in my room, in the tower of the castle,
    young and beautiful and in love and waiting for you with
confidence
    but the princess looks into her mirror and only sees the princess,
while I'm out here, slogging through the mud, breathing fire,
                                and getting stabbed to death.
                    Okay, so I'm the dragon. Big deal.
        You still get to be the hero.
You get magic gloves! A fish that talks! You get eyes like flashlights!
        What more do you want?
I make you pancakes, I take you hunting, I talk to you as if you're
    really there.
Are you there, sweetheart? Do you know me? Is this microphone live?
            Let me do it right for once,
    for the record, let me make a thing of cream and stars that becomes,
you know the story, simply heaven.
        Inside your head you hear a phone ringing
                    and when you open your eyes
only a clearing with deer in it. Hello deer.
        Inside your head the sound of glass,
a car crash sound as the trucks roll over and explode in slow motion.
    Hello darling, sorry about that.
                Sorry about the bony elbows, sorry we
lived here, sorry about the scene at the bottom of the stairwell
            and how I ruined everything by saying it out loud.
    Especially that, but I should have known.
You see, I take the parts that I remember and stitch them back together
    to make a creature that will do what I say
or love me back.
        I'm not really sure why I do it, but in this version you are *not*
feeding yourself to a bad man
                against a black sky prickled with small lights.
    I take it back.
The wooden halls like caskets. These terms from the lower depths.
        I take them back.

Here is the repeated image of the lover destroyed.

                              Crossed out.
      Clumsy hands in a dark room. Crossed out. There is something
underneath the floorboards.

        Crossed out. And here is the tabernacle

                          reconstructed.
Here is the part where everyone was happy all the time and we were all
      forgiven,
even though we didn't deserve it.

                        Inside your head you hear
a phone ringing, and when you open your eyes you're washing up
      in a stranger's bathroom,
standing by the window in a yellow towel, only twenty minutes away
            from the dirtiest thing you know.
All the rooms of the castle except this one, says someone, and suddenly
                              darkness,
                        suddenly only darkness.
In the living room, in the broken yard,
            in the back of the car as the lights go by. In the airport
      bathroom's gurgle and flush, bathed in a pharmacy of
unnatural light,
      my hands looking weird, my face weird, my feet too far away.
And then the airplane, the window seat over the wing with a view
                  of the wing and a little foil bag of peanuts.
I arrived in the city and you met me at the station,
      smiling in a way
            that made me frightened. Down the alley, around the arcade,
      up the stairs of the building
to the little room with the broken faucets, your drawings, all your things.
                  I looked out the window and said
            This doesn't look that much different from home,
      because it didn't,
but then I noticed the black sky and all those lights.
                  We walked through the house to the elevated train.
      All these buildings, all that glass and the shiny beautiful

mechanical wind.

We were inside the train car when I started to cry. You were crying too,
    smiling and crying in a way that made me
even more hysterical. You said I could have anything I wanted, but I
                                    just couldn't say it out loud.

Actually, you said *Love, for you,*
                is larger than the usual romantic love. It's like a religion. It's
                                    terrifying. No one
                        will ever want to sleep with you.

Okay, if you're so great, you do it—
        here's the pencil, make it work . . .

If the window is on your right, you are in your own bed. If the window
    is over your heart, and it is painted shut, then we are breathing
river water.

        Build me a city and call it Jerusalem. Build me another and call it
                                    Jerusalem.

            We have come back from Jerusalem where we found not
what we sought, so do it over, give me another version,
    a different room, another hallway, the kitchen painted over
and over,
        another bowl of soup.

The entire history of human desire takes about seventy minutes to tell.
    Unfortunately, we don't have that kind of time.

                            Forget the dragon,
leave the gun on the table, this has nothing to do with happiness.

                Let's jump ahead to the moment of epiphany,
        in gold light, as the camera pans to where
the action is,
        lakeside and backlit, and it all falls into frame, close enough to see
                the blue rings of my eyes as I say
                                something ugly.

I never liked that ending either. More love streaming out the wrong way,
        and I don't want to be the kind that says *the wrong way.*
But it doesn't work, these erasures, this constant refolding of the pleats.
                There were some nice parts, sure,

all lemondrop and mellonball, laughing in silk pajamas
and the grains of sugar
on the toast, *love love* or whatever, take a number. I'm sorry
it's such a lousy story.
Dear Forgiveness, you know that recently
we have had our difficulties and there are many things
I want to ask you.
I tried that one time, high school, second lunch, and then again,
years later, in the chlorinated pool.
I am still talking to you about help. I still do not have
these luxuries.
I have told you where I'm coming from, so put it together.
We clutch our bellies and roll on the floor . . .
When I say this, it should mean laughter,
not poison.
I want more applesauce. I want more seats reserved for heroes.
Dear Forgiveness, I saved a plate for you.
Quit milling around the yard and come inside.

II

Visible World

Sunlight pouring across your skin, your shadow
                          flat on the wall.
     The dawn was breaking the bones of your heart like twigs.
You had not expected this,
        the bedroom gone white, the astronomical light
                  pummeling you in a stream of fists.
    You raised your hand to your face as if
       to hide it, the pink fingers gone gold as the light
streamed straight to the bone,
    as if you were the small room closed in glass
               with every speck of dust illuminated.
    The light is no mystery,
the mystery is that there is something to keep the light
                    from passing through.

Boot Theory

A man walks into a bar and says:
                    Take my wife—please.
                                        So you do.
        You take her out into the rain and you fall in love with her
                            and she leaves you and you're desolate.
You're on your back in your undershirt, a broken man
            on an ugly bedspread, staring at the water stains
                                        on the ceiling.
        And you can hear the man in the apartment above you
                    taking off his shoes.
You hear the first boot hit the floor and you're looking up,
                                        you're waiting
        because you thought it would follow, you thought there would be
                some logic, perhaps, something to pull it all together
        but here we are in the weeds again,
                                        here we are
in the bowels of the thing: your world doesn't make sense.
            And then the second boot falls.
                        And then a third, a fourth, a fifth.

    A man walks into a bar and says:
                    Take my wife—please.
                                But you take him instead.
        You take him home, and you make him a cheese sandwich,
                and you try to get his shoes off, but he kicks you
                                    and he keeps kicking you.
        You swallow a bottle of sleeping pills but they don't work.
            Boots continue to fall to the floor
                                in the apartment above you.
You go to work the next day pretending nothing happened.
            Your co-workers ask
                        if everything's okay and you tell them

you're just tired.
And you're trying to smile. And they're trying to smile.

A man walks into a bar, you this time, and says:
          Make it a double.
    A man walks into a bar, you this time, and says:
                              Walk a mile in my shoes.
A man walks into a convenience store, still you, saying:
        I only wanted something simple, something generic . . .
But the clerk tells you to buy something or get out.
A man takes his sadness down to the river and throws it in the river
        but then he's still left
with the river. A man takes his sadness and throws it away
                  but then he's still left with his hands.

A Primer for the Small Weird Loves

1

The blond boy in the red trunks is holding your head underwater
because he is trying to kill you,
      and you deserve it, you do, and you know this,
              and you are ready to die in this swimming pool
because you wanted to touch his hands and lips and this means
                    your life is over anyway.
      You're in the eighth grade. You know these things.
You know how to ride a dirt bike, and you know how to do
      long division,
and you know that a boy who likes boys is a dead boy, unless
              he keeps his mouth shut, which is what you
                    didn't do,
because you are weak and hollow and it doesn't matter anymore.

2

A dark-haired man in a rented bungalow is licking the whiskey
from the back of your wrist.
      He feels nothing,
          keeps a knife in his pocket,
                  peels an apple right in front of you
      while you tramp around a mustard-colored room
in your underwear
             drinking Dutch beer from a green bottle.
After everything that was going to happen has happened
you ask only for the cab fare home
         and realize you should have asked for more
             because he couldn't care less, either way.

3

The man on top of you is teaching you how to hate, sees you
as a piece of real estate,
>> just another fallow field lying underneath him
>>> like a sacrifice.
He's turning your back into a table so he doesn't have to
eat off the floor, so he can get comfortable,
pressing against you until he fits, until he's made a place for himself
>>>> inside you.
The clock ticks from five to six. Kissing degenerates into biting.
So you get a kidney punch, a little blood in your urine.
>>>> It isn't over yet, it's just begun.

4

Says to himself
> *The boy's no good. The boy is just no good.*
but he takes you in his arms and pushes your flesh around
>> to see if you could ever be ugly to him.
You, the now familiar whipping boy, but you're beautiful,
>>> he can feel the dogs licking his heart.
Who gets the whip and who gets the hoops of flame?
>>> He hits you and he hits you and he hits you.
Desire driving his hands right into your body.
> *Hush, my sweet. These tornadoes are for you.*
You wanted to think of yourself as someone who did these kinds of things.
>> You wanted to be in love
>>> and he happened to get in the way.

5

The green-eyed boy in the powder-blue t-shirt standing
next to you in the supermarket recoils as if hit,
>> repeatedly, by a lot of men, as if he has a history of it.

This is not your problem.

                 You have your own body to deal with.

The lamp by the bed is broken.

You are feeling things he's no longer in touch with.

         And everyone is speaking softly,

                 so as not to wake one another.

The wind knocks the heads of the flowers together.

          Steam rises from every cup at every table at once.

Things happen all the time, things happen every minute

               that have nothing to do with us.

6

So you say you want a deathbed scene, the knowledge that comes

       before knowledge,

           and you want it dirty.

       And no one can ever figure out what you want,

                and you won't tell them,

and you realize the one person in the world who loves you

           isn't the one you thought it would be,

    and you don't trust him to love you in a way

                you would enjoy.

        And the boy who loves you the wrong way is filthy.

And the boy who loves you the wrong way keeps weakening.

     You thought if you handed over your body

              he'd do something interesting.

7

The stranger says there are no more couches and he will have to

     sleep in your bed. You try to warn him, you tell him

          you will want to get inside him, and ruin him,

    but he doesn't listen.

You do this, you do. You take the things you love

             and tear them apart

or you pin them down with your body and pretend they're yours.
So, you kiss him, and he doesn't move, he doesn't
pull away, and you keep on kissing him. And he hasn't moved,
he's frozen, and you've kissed him, and he'll never
forgive you, and maybe now he'll leave you alone.

Unfinished Duet

At first there were too many branches
so he cut them and then it was winter.
He meaning you. Yes. He would look out
the window and stare at the trees that once
had too many branches and now seemed
to have too few. *Is that all?* No, there were
other attempts, breakfasts: plates served,
plates carried away. *He doesn't know
what to do with his hands.* He likes the feel
of the coffeepot. *More than the hacksaw?*
Yes, and he likes flipping the chairs,
watching them fill with people. He likes
the orange juice and toast of it, and waxed
floors in any light. *He wants to be tender
and merciful.* That sounds overly valorous.
Sounds like penance. And his hands?
His hands keep turning into birds and
flying away from him. *Him being you.*
Yes. *Do you love yourself?* I don't have to
answer that. *It should matter.* He has a
body but it doesn't matter, clean sheets
on the bed but it doesn't matter. *This is
where he trots out his sadness. Little black
cloud, little black umbrella.* You miss
the point: the face in the mirror is a little
traitor, the face in the mirror is a pale
and naked hostage and no one can tell
which room he's being held in. *He wants
in, he wants out, he wants the antidote.
He stands in front of the mirror with a net,
hoping to catch something.* He wants to
move forward into the afternoon because

there is no other choice. *Everyone in this
room got here somehow and everyone in
this room will have to leave.* So what's left?
Sing a song about the room we're in?
Hammer in the pegs that fix the meaning
to the landscape? *The voice wants to be
a hand and the hand wants to do something
useful. What did you really want?* Someone
to pass this with me. *You wanted more.*
I want what everyone wants. *He raises
the moon on a crane for effect, cue the violins.*
That's what the violins are for. And yes,
he raises the moon on a crane and scrubs it
until it shines. *So what does it shine on?*
Nothing. *Was there no one else?* Left-handed
truth, right-handed truth, there's no pure
way to say it. *The wind blows and it makes
a noise. Pain makes a noise. We bang on
the pipes and it makes a noise. Was there
no one else?* His hands keep turning into
birds, and his hands keep flying away
from him. *Eventually the birds must land.*

I Had a Dream About You

All the cows were falling out of the sky and landing in the mud.
You were drinking sangria and I was throwing oranges at you,
                                                but it didn't matter.
        I said my arms are very long and your head's on fire.
    I said kiss me here and here and here
                    and you did.
                            Then you wanted pasta,
so we trampled out into the tomatoes and rolled around to make the sauce.
    You were very beautiful.

We were in the Safeway parking lot. I couldn't find my cigarettes.
            You said *Hurry up!* but I was worried there would be a holdup
and we would be stuck in a hostage situation, hiding behind
                    the frozen meats, with nothing to smoke for hours.
        You said *Don't be silly*,
            so I followed you into the store.
We were thumping the melons when I heard somebody say *Nobody move!*
            I leaned over and whispered in your ear *I told you so.*

        There was a show on the television about buried treasure.
You were trying to convince me that we should buy shovels
                            and go out into the yard
        and I was trying to convince you that I was a vampire.
On the way to the hardware store I kept biting your arm
        and you said if I really was a vampire I would be biting your neck,
                so I started biting your neck
                        and you said *Cut it out!*
and you bought me an ice cream, and then we saw the UFO.

These are the dreams we should be having. I shouldn't have to
                        clean them up like this.

You were lying in the middle of the empty highway.
The sky was red and the sand was red and you were wearing a brown coat.
There were flecks of foam in the corners of your mouth.
The birds were watching you.
Your eyes were closed and you were listening to the road and I could
hear you breathing, I could hear your heart beating.
I carried you to the car and drove you home but you
weren't making any sense.
I took a shower and tried to catch my breath.
You were lying on top of the bedspread
in boxer shorts, watching cartoons and laughing but not making any sound.
Your skin looked blue in the television light.
Your teeth looked yellow.
Still wet, I lay down next to you. Your arms, your legs, your naked chest,
your ribs delineated like a junkyard dog's.
There's nowhere to go, I thought. *There's nowhere to go.*

You were sitting in a bathtub at the hospital and you were crying.
You said it hurt.
I mean the buildings that were not the hospital.
I shouldn't have mentioned the hospital.
I don't think I can take this much longer.

In the dream I don't tell anyone, you put your head in my lap.
Let's say you're driving down the road with your eyes closed
but my eyes are also closed.
You're by the side of the road.
You're by the side of the road and you're doing all the talking
while I stare at my shoes.
They're nice shoes, brown and comfortable, and I like your voice.
In the dream I don't tell anyone, I'm afraid to wake you up.

In these dreams it's always you:
the boy in the sweatshirt,

the boy on the bridge, the boy who always keeps me

from jumping off the bridge.

Oh, the things we invent when we are scared

and want to be rescued.

Your jeep. Your teeth. The coffee that you bought me.

The sandwich cut in half on the plate.

I woke up and ate ice cream in the dark,

hunched over on the wooden chair in the kitchen,

listening to the rain.

I borrowed your shoes and didn't put them away.

You were crying and eating rice.

The surface of the water was still and bright.

Your feet were burning so I put my hands on them, but my hands

were burning too.

You had a bottle of pills but I wouldn't let you swallow them.

You said *Will you love me even more when I'm dead?*

and I said *No*, and I threw the pills on the sand.

Look at them, you said. *They look like emeralds.*

I put you in a cage with the ocelots. I was trying to fatten you up

with sausages and bacon.

Somehow you escaped and climbed up the branches of a pear tree.

I chopped it down but there was nobody in it.

I went to the riverbed to wait for you to show up.

You didn't show up.

I kept waiting.

Straw House, Straw Dog

1

I watched TV.   I had a Coke at the bar.   I had four dreams in a row
where you were burned, about to burn, or still on fire.
          I watched TV.   I had a Coke at the bar. I had four Cokes,
four dreams in a row.

Here you are in the straw house, feeding the straw dog. Here you are
          in the wrong house, feeding the wrong dog. I had a Coke with ice.
I had four dreams on TV.   You have a cold cold smile.
          You were burned, you were about to burn, you're still on fire.

Here you are in the straw house, feeding ice to the dog, and you wanted
          an adventure, so I said   *Have an adventure.*
The straw about to burn, the straw on fire. Here you are on the TV,
          saying *Watch me, just watch me.*

2

Four dreams in a row, four dreams in a row, four dreams in a row,
          fall down right there. I wanted to fall down right there but I knew
you wouldn't catch me because you're dead.   I swallowed crushed ice
pretending it was glass and you're dead. Ashes to ashes.

You wanted to be cremated so we cremated you and you wanted an adventure
          so I ran   and I knew you wouldn't catch me.
You are a fever I am learning to live with, and everything is happening
          at the wrong end of a very long tunnel.

3

I woke up in the morning and I didn't want anything, didn't do anything,
          couldn't do it anyway,

just lay there listening to the blood rush through me and it never made
      any sense, anything.

And I can't eat, can't sleep, can't sit still or fix things and I wake up and I
wake up and you're still dead, you're under the table, you're still feeding
      the damn dog, you're cutting the room in half.
Whatever.   Feed him whatever.   Burn the straw house down.

4

I don't really blame you for being dead but you can't have your sweater back.
      So, I said, *now that we have our dead, what are we going to do with them?*
There's a black dog and there's a white dog, depends on which you feed,
      depends on which damn dog you live with.

5

Here we are
      in the wrong tunnel, burn O burn, but it's cold, I have clothes
all over my body, and it's raining, it wasn't supposed to. And there's snow
      on the TV, a landscape full of snow, falling from the fire-colored sky.

But thanks, thanks for calling it   *the blue sky*
      You can sleep now, you said. You can sleep now. You said that.
I had a dream where you said that. Thanks for saying that.
      You weren't supposed to.

Saying Your Names

Chemical names, bird names, names of fire
and flight and snow, baby names, paint names,
delicate names like bones in the body,
Rumplestiltskin names that are always changing,
names that no one's ever able to figure out.
Names of spells and names of hexes, names
cursed quietly under the breath, or called out
loudly to fill the yard, calling you inside again,
calling you home. Nicknames and pet names
and baroque French monikers, written in
shorthand, written in longhand, scrawled
illegibly in brown ink on the backs of yellowing
photographs, or embossed on envelopes lined
with gold. Names called out across the water,
names I called you behind your back,
sour and delicious, secret and unrepeatable,
the names of flowers that open only once,
shouted from balconies, shouted from rooftops,
or muffled by pillows, or whispered in sleep,
or caught in the throat like a lump of meat.
I try, I do. I try and try. A happy ending?
Sure enough—*Hello darling, welcome home.*
I'll call you darling, hold you tight. We are
not traitors but the lights go out. It's dark.
Sweetheart, is that you? There are no tears,
no pictures of him squarely. A seaside framed
in glass, and boats, those little boats with
sails aflutter, shining lights upon the water,
lights that splinter when they hit the pier.
His voice on tape, his name on the envelope,
the soft sound of a body falling off a bridge
behind you, the body hardly even makes

a sound. The waters of the dead, a clear road,
every lover in the form of stars, the road
blocked. All night I stretched my arms across
him, rivers of blood, the dark woods, singing
with all my skin and bone *Please keep him safe.*
Let him lay his head on my chest and we will be
like sailors, swimming in the sound of it, dashed
to pieces. Makes a cathedral, him pressing against
me, his lips at my neck, and yes, I do believe
his mouth is heaven, his kisses falling over me
like stars. Names of heat and names of light,
names of collision in the dark, on the side of the
bus, in the bark of the tree, in ballpoint pen
on jeans and hands and the backs of matchbooks
that then get lost. Names like pain cries, names
like tombstones, names forgotten and reinvented,
names forbidden or overused. Your name like
a song I sing to myself, your name like a box
where I keep my love, your name like a nest
in the tree of love, your name like a boat in the
sea of love—O now we're in the sea of love!
Your name like detergent in the washing machine.
Your name like two X's like punched-in eyes,
like a drunk cartoon passed out in the gutter,
your name with two X's to mark the spots,
to hold the place, to keep the treasure from
becoming ever lost. I'm saying your name
in the grocery store, I'm saying your name on
the bridge at dawn. Your name like an animal
covered with frost, your name like a music that's
been transposed, a suit of fur, a coat of mud,
a kick in the pants, a lungful of glass, the sails
in wind and the slap of waves on the hull
of a boat that's sinking to the sound of mermaids
singing songs of love, and the tug of a simple

profound sadness when it sounds so far away.
Here is a map with your name for a capital,
here is an arrow to prove a point: we laugh
and it pits the world against us, we laugh,
and we've got nothing left to lose, and our hearts
turn red, and the river rises like a barn on fire.
I came to tell you, we'll swim in the water, we'll
swim like something sparkling underneath
the waves. Our bodies shivering, and the sound
of our breathing, and the shore so far away.
I'll use my body like a ladder, climbing
to the thing behind it, saying farewell to flesh,
farewell to everything caught underfoot
and flattened. Names of poisons, names of
handguns, names of places we've been
together, names of people we'd be together.
Names of endurance, names of devotion,
street names and place names and all the names
of our dark heaven crackling in their pan.
It's a bed of straw, darling. It sure as shit is.
If there was one thing I could save from the fire,
he said, *the broken arms of the sycamore,*
the eucalyptus still trying to climb out of the yard—
your breath on my neck like a music that holds
my hands down, kisses as they burn their way
along my spine—or rain, our bodies wet,
clothes clinging arm to elbow, clothes clinging
nipple to groin—I'll be right here. I'm waiting.
Say hallelujah, say goodnight, say it over
the canned music and your feet won't stumble,
his face getting larger, the rest blurring
on every side. And angels, about twelve angels,
angels knocking on your head right now, hello
hello, a flash in the sky, would you like to
meet him there, in Heaven? Imagine a room,

a sudden glow. Here is my hand, my heart,
my throat, my wrist. Here are the illuminated
cities at the center of me, and here is the center
of me, which is a lake, which is a well that we
can drink from, but I can't go through with it.
I just don't want to die anymore.

III

Planet of Love

Imagine this:
You're driving.
      The sky's bright. You look great.
            In a word, in a phrase, it's a movie,
                        you're the star,
so smile for the camera, it's your big scene,
      you know your lines.
                    I'm the director. I'm in a helicopter.
           I have a megaphone and you play along,
                   because you want to die for love,
              you always have.
Imagine this:
You're pulling the car over. Somebody's waiting.
      You're going to die
           in your best friend's arms.
And you play along because it's funny, because it's written down,
you've memorized it,
      it's all you know.
           I say the phrases that keep it all going,
                and everybody plays along.
   Imagine:
Someone's pulling a gun, and you're jumping into the middle of it.
      You didn't think you'd feel this way.
There's a gun in your hand.
      It feels hot. It feels oily.

      I'm the director
and I'm screaming at you,
      I'm waving my arms in the sky,
           and everyone's watching, everyone's
                curious, everyone's
            holding their breath.

Wishbone

You saved my life he says. *I owe you, I owe you everything.*
You don't, I say, you don't owe me squat, let's just get going, let's just
       get gone, but he's relentless,
keeps saying *I owe you*, says *Your shoes are filling with your own*
damn blood, you must want something, just tell me, and it's yours.
       But I can't look at him, can hardly speak:
I took the bullet for all the wrong reasons, I'd just as soon kill you myself,
I say. You keep saying *I owe you, I owe* . . . but you say the same thing
       every time. Let's not talk about it, let's just not talk.
Not because I don't believe it, not because I want it any different, but I'm
always saving and you're always owing and I'm tired of asking to settle
       the debt. Don't bother. You never mean it
anyway, not really, and it only makes me that much more ashamed.
There's only one thing I want, don't make me say it, just get me bandages,
       I'm bleeding, I'm not just making conversation.
There's smashed glass glittering everywhere like stars. It's a Western,
Henry. It's a downright shoot-em-up. We've made a graveyard
       out of the bone white afternoon.
It's another wrong-man-dies scenario, and we keep doing it Henry,
keep saying *until we get it right* . . . but we always win and we never quit.
       See, we've won again,
here we are at the place where I get to beg for it, where I get to say *Please,*
for just one night, will you lie down next to me, we can leave our clothes on,
       we can stay all buttoned up . . .
But we both know how it goes—I say *I want you inside me* and you hold
my head underwater, I say *I want you inside me* and you split me open
       with a knife.
I'm battling monsters, I'm pulling you out of the burning buildings
and you say *I'll give you anything* but you never come through.
       Even when you're standing up
you look like you're lying down, but will you let me kiss your neck, baby?

Do I have to tie your arms down? Do I have to stick my tongue in your
          mouth like the hand of a thief,
like a burglary, like it's just another petty theft? It makes me tired,
Henry. Do you see what I mean? Do you see what I'm getting at?
          I swear, I end up
feeling empty, like you've taken something out of me, and I have to search
my body for the scars, thinking *Did he find that one last tender place to
          sink his teeth in?*
I know you want me to say it, Henry, it's in the script, you want me to say
Lie down on the bed, you're all I ever wanted and worth dying for, too . . .
          but I think I'd rather keep the bullet.
It's mine, see, I'm not giving it up. This way you still owe me, and that's
as good as anything. You can't get out of this one, Henry, you can't get it
          out of me, and with this bullet lodged in my chest,
covered with your name, I will turn myself into a gun, because I'm hungry
and hollow and just want something to call my own. I'll be your
          slaughterhouse, your killing floor, your morgue
and final resting, walking around with this bullet inside me like the bullet
was already there, like it's been waiting inside me the whole time.
          Do you want it? Do you want anything I have?
Will you throw me to the ground like you mean it, reach inside and wrestle
it out with your bare hands? If you love me, Henry, you don't love me
          in a way I understand.
Do you know how it ends? Do you feel lucky? Do you want to go home
now? There's a bottle of whiskey in the trunk of the Chevy and a
          dead man at our feet
staring up at us like we're something interesting. This is where the evening
splits in half, Henry, love or death. Grab an end, pull hard,
          and make a wish.

Driving, Not Washing

It starts with bloodshed, always bloodshed, always the same
                    running from something larger than yourself story,
shoving money into the jaws of a suitcase, cutting your hair
        with a steak knife at a rest stop,
and you're off, you're on the run, a fugitive driving away from
                            something shameful and half-remembered.
They're hurling their bodies down the freeway
                        to the smell of gasoline,
    which is the sound of a voice saying I told you so.
                                    Yes, you did dear.
Every story has its chapter in the desert, the long slide from kingdom
        to kingdom through the wilderness,
                where you learn things, where you're left to your own devices.
Henry's driving,
        and Theodore's bleeding shotgun into the upholstery.
It's a road movie,
            a double-feature, two boys striking out across America, while desire,
                like a monster, crawls up out of the lake
with all of us watching, with all of us wondering if these two boys will
        find a way to figure it out.
                        Here is the black box, the shut eye,
the bullet pearling in his living skin. This boy, half-destroyed,
        screaming *Drive into that tree, drive off the embankment.*
                        Henry, make something happen.
But angels are pouring out of the farmland, angels are swarming
            over the grassland,
Angels rising from their little dens, arms swinging, wings aflutter,
        dropping their white-hot bombs of love.
                We are not dirty, he keeps saying. *We are not dirty . . .*
        They want you to love the whole damn world but you won't,
you want it all narrowed down to one fleshy man in the bath,

who knows what to do with his body, with his hands.
It should follow,
   you know this, like the panels of a comic strip,
      we should be belted in, but you still can't get beyond your skin,
and they're trying to drive you into the ground, to see if anything
                walks away.

Road Music

1

The eye stretches to the horizon and then must continue up.

Anything past the horizon

is invisible, it can only be imagined. You want to see the future but
you only see the sky. Fluffy clouds.

Look—white fluffy clouds.

Looking back is easy for a while and then looking back gets
murky. There is the road, and there is the story of where the road goes,
and then more road,
the roar of the freeway, the roar of the city sheening across the city.

There should be a place.

At the rest stop, in the restaurant, the overpass, the water's edge . . .

2

He was not dead yet, not exactly—

parts of him were dead already, certainly other parts were still only waiting
for something to happen, something grand, but it isn't

always about me,

he keeps saying, though he's talking about the only heart he knows—

He could build a city. Has a certain capacity. There's a niche in his chest
where a heart would fit perfectly

and he thinks if he could just maneuver one into place—

well then, game over.

3

You wonder what he's thinking when he shivers like that.

What can you tell me, what could you possibly
tell me? Sure, it's good to feel things, and if it hurts, we're doing it

to ourselves, or so the saying goes, but there should be
a different music here. There should be just one safe place
in the world, I mean
this world. People get hurt here. People fall down and stay down and I don't like
the way the song goes.
You, the moon. You, the road. You, the little flowers
by the side of the road. You keep singing along to that song I hate. Stop singing.

The Dislocated Room

It was night for many miles and then the real stars in the purple sky,
   like little boats rowed out too far,
begin to disappear.
            And there, in the distance, not the promised land,
                              but a Holiday Inn,
with bougainvillea growing through the chain link by the pool.
   The door swung wide: twin beds, twin lamps, twin plastic cups
wrapped up in cellophane
            and he says *No Henry, let's not do this.*
Can you see the plot like dotted lines across the room?
   Here is the sink to wash away the blood,
here's the whiskey, the ripped-up shirt. Here is the tile of the bathroom
      floor, the disk of the drain
                  punched through with holes.
Here is the boy like a sack of meat, here are the engines, the little room
   that is not a room,
the Henry that is not a Henry, the Henry with a needle and thread,
      hovering over the hollow boy passed out
                        on the universal bedspread.
         Here he is again, being sewn up.
So now we have come to a great battlefield, the warmth of the fire,
   the fire still burning,
                  the heat escaping like a broken promise.
      This is the part where you wake up in your clothes again,
this is the part where you're trying to stay inside the building.
      Stay in the room for now, he says. *Stay in the room*
                              for now.

This is the place, you say to yourself, where everything
   starts to begin,
the wounds reveal a thicker skin and suddenly there is no floor.
                        Meanwhile,

there is something underneath the building that is trying very hard
                        to get your attention—
    a man with almond eyes and a zipper that runs the length
                                              of his spine.
You can see the shadow that the man is throwing across
        the linoleum,
how it resembles a boat, how it crosses the tiles just so,
                the masts of his arms rasping against the windows.
He's pointing at you with a glass of milk
            as if he's trying to tell you that there is
some sort of shining star now buried deep inside you and he has to
                                dig it out with a knife.
        The bell rings, the dog growls,
and then the wind picking up, and the light falling,
            and the window closing tight against the dirty rain.
Here is the hallway and here are the doors and here is the fear of the
        other thing, the relentless
                        thing, your body drowning in gravity.
This is the in-between, the waiting that happens in the
        space between
one note and the next, the part where you confuse
                            his hands with the room, the dog
        with the man, the blood
                                with the ripped-up sky.
He puts his hands all over you to keep you in the room.
            It's night. It's noon. He's driving. It's happening
    all over again.
                        It's love or it isn't. It isn't over.
You're in a car. You're in the weeds again. You're on a bumpy road
                and there are criminals everywhere,
                                    longing for danger.
            Henry, he's saying. *Who is it that's talking?*
I thought I heard the clink
            of ice to teeth. I thought I heard the clink of teeth to glass.

Open the door and the light falls in. Open your mouth and it falls
    right out again.
He's on top of you. He's next to you, right next to you in fact.
            He has the softest skin wrapped entirely around him.
                                                        It isn't him.
It isn't you. You're falling now. You're swimming. This is not
    harmless. You are not
            breathing. You're climbing out of the chlorinated pool again.
We have not been given all the words necessary.
                    We have not been given anything at all.
        We've been driving all night.
                            We've been driving a long time.
            We want to stop. We can't.
Is there an acceptable result? Do we mean something when we talk?
        Is it enough that we are shuddering
                                    from the sound?
Left hand raising the fork to the mouth, feeling the meat slide down
    your throat, thinking
            My throat. Mine. Everything in this cone of light is mine.
The ashtray and the broken lamp, the filthy orange curtains and his
    ruined shirt.
                I've been in your body, baby, and it was paradise.
    I've been in your body and it was a carnival ride.
They want to stop but they can't stop. They don't know what
                                            they're doing.
This is not harmless, the *how to touch it*, we do not want the screen
    completely
lifted from our eyes, just lifted long enough to see the holes.
        Tired and sore and rubbed the wrong way,
                rubbed raw and throbbing in the light.
They want to stop but they don't stop. They cannot get the bullet out.
        Cut me open and the light streams out.
    Stitch me up and the light keeps streaming out between
                                    the stitches.

He cannot get the bullet out, he thinks, he can't, and then, he does.
    A little piece of grit to build a pearl around.
Midnight June. Midnight July. They've been going at it for days now.
   Getting the bullet out.
Digging out the bullet and holding it up to the light, the light.
           Digging out the bullet and holding it up to the light.

You Are Jeff

1

There are two twins on motorbikes but one is farther up the road, beyond the hairpin turn, or just before it, depending on which twin you are in love with at the time. Do not choose sides yet. It is still to your advantage to remain impartial. Both motorbikes are shiny red and both boys have perfect teeth, dark hair, soft hands. The one in front will want to take you apart, and slowly. His deft and stubby fingers searching every shank and lock for weaknesses. You could love this boy with all your heart. The other brother only wants to stitch you back together. The sun shines down. It's a beautiful day. Consider the hairpin turn. Do not choose sides yet.

2

There are two twins on motorbikes but one is farther up the road. Let's call them Jeff. And because the first Jeff is in front we'll consider him the older, and therefore responsible for lending money and the occasional punch in the shoulder. World-wise, world-weary, and not his mother's favorite, this Jeff will always win when it all comes down to fisticuffs. Unfortunately for him, it doesn't always all come down to fisticuffs. Jeff is thinking about his brother down the winding road behind him. He is thinking that if only he could cut him open and peel him back and crawl inside this second skin, then he could relive that last mile again: reborn, wild-eyed, free.

3

There are two twins on motorbikes but one is farther up the road, beyond the hairpin turn, or just before it, depending on which Jeff you are. It could have been so beautiful—you scout out the road ahead and I will watch your back, how it was and how it will be, memory and fantasy—but each Jeff wants to be the other one. My name is Jeff and I'm tired of looking at the back of your head. My name is Jeff and I'm tired of seeing my hand me down clothes. Look, Jeff, I'm telling you, for the last time, I mean it, etcetera. They are the same and they are not the same. They are the same and they hate each other for it.

4

Your name is Jeff and somewhere up ahead of you your brother has pulled to the side of the road and he is waiting for you with a lug wrench clutched in his greasy fist. O how he loves you, darling boy. O how, like always, he invents the monsters underneath the bed to get you to sleep next to him, chest to chest or chest to back, the covers drawn around you in an act of faith against the night. When he throws the wrench into the air it will catch the light as it spins toward you. Look—it looks like a star. You had expected something else, anything else, but the wrench never reaches you. It hangs in the air like that, spinning in the air like that. It's beautiful.

5

Let's say God in his High Heaven is hungry and has decided to make himself some tuna fish sandwiches. He's already finished making two of them, on sourdough, before he realizes that the fish is bad. What is he going to do with these sandwiches? They're already made, but he doesn't want to eat them.

Let's say the Devil is played by two men. We'll call them Jeff. Dark hair, green eyes, white teeth, pink tongues—they're twins. The one on the left has gone bad in the middle, and the other one on the left is about to. As they wrestle, you can tell that they have forgotten about God, and they are very hungry.

6

You are playing cards with three men named Jeff. Two of the Jeffs seem somewhat familiar, but the Jeff across from you keeps staring at your hands, your mouth, and you're certain that you've never seen this Jeff before. But he's on your team, and you're ahead, you're winning big, and yet the other Jeffs keep smiling at you like there's no tomorrow. They all have perfect teeth: white, square, clean, even. And, for some reason, the lighting in the room makes their teeth seem closer than they should be, as if each mouth was a place, a living room with pink carpet and the window's open. *Come back from the window, Jefferson. Take off those wet clothes and come over here, by the fire.*

7

You are playing cards with three Jeffs. One is your father, one is your brother, and the other is your current boyfriend. All of them have seen you naked and heard you talking in your sleep. Your boyfriend Jeff gets up to answer the phone. To them he is a mirror, but to you he is a room. *Phone's for you,* Jeff says. Hey! It's Uncle Jeff, who isn't really your uncle, but you can't talk right now, one of the Jeffs has put his tongue in your mouth. Please let it be the right one.

8

Two brothers are fighting by the side of the road. Two motorbikes have fallen over on the shoulder, leaking oil into the dirt, while the interlocking brothers grapple and swing. You see them through the backseat window as you and your parents drive past. You are twelve years old. You do not have a brother. You have never experienced anything this ferocious or intentional with another person. Your mother is pretending that she hasn't seen anything. Your father is fiddling with the knobs of the radio. There is an empty space next to you in the backseat of the station wagon. Make it the shape of everything you need. Now say hello.

9

You are in an ordinary suburban bedroom with bunk beds, a bookshelf, two wooden desks and chairs. You are lying on your back, on the top bunk, very close to the textured ceiling, staring straight at it in fact, and the room is still dark except for a wedge of powdery light that spills in from the adjoining bathroom. The bathroom is covered in mint green tile and someone is in there, singing very softly. Is he singing to you? For you? Black cherries in chocolate, the ring around the moon, a beetle underneath a glass—you cannot make out all the words, but you're sure he knows you're in there, and he's singing to you, even though you don't know who he is.

10

You see it as a room, a tabernacle, the dark hotel. You're in the hallway again, and you open the door, and if you're ready you'll see it, but maybe one part of your mind decides that the other parts aren't ready, and then you don't remember where you've been, and you find yourself down the hall again, the lights gone dim as the left hand sings the right hand back to sleep. It's a puzzle: each piece, each room, each time you put your hand to the knob, your mouth to the hand, your ear to the wound that whispers.

You're in the hallway again. The radio is playing your favorite song. You're in the hallway. Open the door again. Open the door.

11

Suppose for a moment that the heart has two heads, that the heart has been chained and dunked in a glass booth filled with river water. The heart is monologing about hesitation and fulfillment while behind the red brocade the heart is drowning. Can the heart escape? Does love even care? Snow falls as we dump the booth in the bay.

Suppose for a moment we are crowded around a pier, waiting for something to ripple the water. *We believe in you. There is no danger. It is not getting dark,* we want to say.

12

Consider the hairpin turn. It is waiting for you like a red door or the broken leg of a dog. The sun is shining, O how the sun shines down! Your speedometer and your handgrips and the feel of the road below you, how it knows you, the black ribbon spread out on the greens between these lines that suddenly don't reach to the horizon. It is waiting, like a broken door, like the red dog that chases its tail and eats your rosebushes and then must be forgiven. Who do you love, Jeff? Who do you love? You were driving toward something and then, well, then you found yourself driving the other way. The dog is asleep. The road is behind you. O how the sun shines down.

13

This time everyone has the best intentions. You have cancer. Let's say you have cancer. Let's say you've swallowed a bad thing and now it's got its hands inside you. This is the essence of love and failure. You see what I mean but you're happy anyway, and that's okay, it's a love story after all, a lasting love, a wonderful adventure with lots of action, where the mirror says mirror and the hand says hand and the front door never says Sorry Charlie. So the doctor says you need more stitches and the bruise cream isn't working. So much for the facts. Let's say you're still completely in the dark but we love you anyway. We love you. We really do.

14

After work you go to the grocery store to get some milk and a carton of cigarettes. Where did you get those bruises? You don't remember. Work was boring. You find a jar of bruise cream and a can of stewed tomatoes. Maybe a salad? Spinach, walnuts, blue cheese, apples, and you can't decide between the Extra Large or Jumbo black olives. Which is bigger anyway? Extra Large has a blue label, Jumbo has a purple label. Both cans cost $1.29. While you're deciding, the afternoon light is streaming through the windows behind the bank of checkout counters. Take the light inside you like a blessing, like a knee in the chest, holding onto it and not letting it go. Now let it go.

15

Like sandpaper, the light, or a blessing, or a bruise. Blood everywhere, he said, the red light hemorrhaging from everywhere at once. The train station blue, your lips blue, hands cold and the blue wind. Or a horse, your favorite horse now raised up again out of the mud and galloping galloping always toward you. In your ruined shirt, on the last day, while the bruise won't heal, and the stain stays put, the red light streaming in from everywhere at once. Your broken ribs, the back of your head, your hand to mouth or hand to now, right now, like you mean it, like it's splitting you in two. Now look at the lights, the lights.

16

You and your lover are making out in the corner booth of a seedy bar. The booths are plush and the drinks are cheap and in this dim and smoky light you can barely tell whose hands are whose. Someone raises their glass for a toast. Is that the Hand of Judgment or the Hand of Mercy? The bartender smiles, running a rag across the burnished wood of the bar. The drink in front of you has already been paid for. *Drink it,* the bartender says. *It's yours, you deserve it. It's already been paid for. Somebody's paid for it already. There's no mistake,* he says. *It's your drink, the one you asked for, just the way you like it. How can you refuse?* Hands of fire, hands of air, hands of water, hands of dirt. Someone's doing all the talking but no one's lips move. Consider the hairpin turn.

17

The motorbikes are neck and neck but where's the checkered flag we all expected, waving in the distance, telling you you're home again, home? He's next to you, right next to you in fact, so close, or . . . he isn't. Imagine a room. Yes, imagine a room: two chairs facing the window but nobody moves. Don't move. Keep staring straight into my eyes. It feels like you're not moving, the way when, dancing, the room will suddenly fall away. You're dancing: you're neck and neck or cheek to cheek, he's there or he isn't, the open road. Imagine a room. Imagine you're dancing. Imagine the room now falling away. Don't move.

18

Two brothers: one of them wants to take you apart. Two brothers: one of them wants to put you back together. It's time to choose sides now. The stitches or the devouring mouth? You want an alibi? You don't get an alibi, you get two brothers. Here are two Jeffs. Pick one. This is how you make the meaning, you take two things and try to define the space between them. Jeff or Jeff? Who do you want to be? You just wanted to play in your own backyard, but you don't know where your own yard is, exactly. You just wanted to prove there was one safe place, just one safe place where you could love him. You have not found that place yet. You have not made that place yet. You are here. You are here. You're still right here.

19

Here are your names and here is the list and here are the things you left behind: The mark on the floor from pushing your chair back, your underwear, one half brick of cheese, the kind I don't like, wrapped up, and poorly, and abandoned on the second shelf next to the poppyseed dressing, which is also yours. Here's the champagne on the floor, and here are your house keys, and here are the curtains that your cat peed on. And here is your cat, who keeps eating grass and vomiting in the hallway. Here is the list with all of your names, Jeff. They're not the same name, Jeff. They're not the same at all.

20

There are two twins on motorbikes but they are not on motorbikes, they're in a garden where the flowers are as big as thumbs. Imagine you are in a field of daisies. What are you doing in a field of daisies? Get up! Let's say you're not in the field anymore. Let's say they're not brothers anymore. That's right, they're not brothers, they're just one guy, and he knows you, and he's talking to you, but you're in pain and you cannot understand him. What are you still doing in this field? Get out of the field! You should be in the hotel room! You should, at least, be trying to get back into the hotel room. Ah! Now the field is empty.

21

Hold onto your voice. Hold onto your breath. Don't make a noise, don't leave the room until I come back from the dead for you. I will come back from the dead for you. This could be a city. This could be a graveyard. This could be the basket of a big balloon. Leave the lights on. Leave a trail of letters like those little knots of bread we used to dream about. We used to dream about them. We used to do a lot of things. Put your hand to the knob, your mouth to the hand, pick up the bread and devour it. I'm in the hallway again, I'm in the hallway. The radio's playing my favorite song. Leave the lights on. Keep talking. I'll keep walking toward the sound of your voice.

22

Someone had a party while you were sleeping but you weren't really sleeping, you were sick, and parts of you were burning, and you couldn't move. Perhaps the party was in your honor. You can't remember. It seems the phone was ringing in the dream you were having but there's no proof. A dish in the sink that might be yours, some clothes on the floor that might belong to someone else. When was the last time you found yourself looking out of this window. Hey! This is a beautiful window! This is a beautiful view! Those trees lined up like that, and the way the stars are spinning over them like that, spinning in the air like that, like wrenches.

23

Let's say that God is the space between two men and the Devil is the space between two men. Here: I'll be all of them—Jeff and Jeff and Jeff and Jeff are standing on the shoulder of the highway, four motorbikes knocked over, two wrenches spinning in the ordinary air. Two of these Jeffs are windows, and two of these Jeffs are doors, and all of these Jeffs are trying to tell you something. Come closer. We'll whisper it in your ear. It's like seeing your face in a bowl of soup, cream of potato, and the eyes shining back like spoons. If we wanted to tell you everything, we would leave more footprints in the snow or kiss you harder. One thing. Come closer. Listen . . .

24

You're in a car with a beautiful boy, and he won't tell you that he loves you, but he loves you. And you feel like you've done something terrible, like robbed a liquor store, or swallowed pills, or shoveled yourself a grave in the dirt, and you're tired. You're in a car with a beautiful boy, and you're trying not to tell him that you love him, and you're trying to choke down the feeling, and you're trembling, but he reaches over and he touches you, like a prayer for which no words exist, and you feel your heart taking root in your body, like you've discovered something you don't even have a name for.

Meanwhile

Driving, dogs barking, how you get used to it, how you make
                              the new streets yours.
Trees outside the window and a big band sound that makes you feel like
        everything's okay,
    a feeling that lasts for one song maybe,
                        the parentheses all clicking shut behind you.
            The way we move through time and space, or only time.
The way it's night for many miles, and then suddenly
                                        it's not, it's breakfast
    and you're standing in the shower for over an hour,
                        holding the bar of soap up to the light.
I will keep watch. I will water the yard.
        Knot the tie and go to work. Unknot the tie and go to sleep.
                        I sleep. I dream. I make up things
    that I would never say. I say them very quietly.
                    The trees in wind, the streetlights on,
        the click and flash of cigarettes
being smoked on the lawn, and just a little kiss before we say goodnight.
    It spins like a wheel inside you: green yellow, green blue,
                              green beautiful green.
    It's simple: it isn't over, it's just begun. It's green. It's still green.

Snow and Dirty Rain

Close your eyes. A lover is standing too close
to focus on. Leave me blurry and fall toward me
with your entire body. Lie under the covers, pretending
to sleep, while I'm in the other room. Imagine
my legs crossed, my hair combed, the shine of my boots
in the slatted light. I'm thinking *My plant, his chair,*
the ashtray that we bought together. I'm thinking *This is where*
we live. When we were little we made houses out of
cardboard boxes. We can do anything. It's not because
our hearts are large, they're not, it's what we
struggle with. The attempt to say *Come over. Bring*
your friends. It's a potluck, I'm making pork chops, I'm making
those long noodles you love so much. My dragonfly,
my black-eyed fire, the knives in the kitchen are singing
for blood, but we are the crossroads, my little outlaw,
and this is the map of my heart, the landscape
after cruelty which is, of course, a garden, which is
a tenderness, which is a room, a lover saying *Hold me*
tight, it's getting cold. We have not touched the stars,
nor are we forgiven, which brings us back
to the hero's shoulders and a gentleness that comes,
not from the absence of violence, but despite
the abundance of it. The lawn drowned, the sky on fire,
the gold light falling backward through the glass
of every room. I'll give you my heart to make a place
for it to happen, evidence of a love that transcends hunger.
Is that too much to expect? That I would name the stars
for you? That I would take you there? The splash
of my tongue melting you like a sugar cube? We've read
the back of the book, we know what's going to happen.
The fields burned, the land destroyed, the lovers left
broken in the brown dirt. And then it's gone.

Makes you sad. All your friends are gone. Goodbye
Goodbye. No more tears. I would like to meet you all
in Heaven. But there's a litany of dreams that happens
somewhere in the middle. Moonlight spilling
on the bathroom floor. A page of the book where we
transcend the story of our lives, past the taco stands
and record stores. Moonlight making crosses
on your body, and me putting my mouth on every one.
We have been very brave, we have wanted to know
the worst, wanted the curtain to be lifted from our eyes.
This dream going on with all of us in it. Penciling in
the bighearted slob. Penciling in his outstretched arms.
Our Father who art in Heaven. Our Father who art buried
in the yard. Someone is digging your grave right now.
Someone is drawing a bath to wash you clean, he said,
so think of the wind, so happy, so warm. It's a fairy tale,
the story underneath the story, sliding down the polished
halls, lightning here and gone. We make these
ridiculous idols so we can pray to what's behind them,
but what happens after we get up the ladder?
Do we simply stare at what is horrible and forgive it?
Here is the river, and here is the box, and here are
the monsters we put in the box to test our strength
against. Here is the cake, and here is the fork, and here's
the desire to put it inside us, and then the question
behind every question: *What happens next?*
The way you slam your body into mine reminds me
I'm alive, but monsters are always hungry, darling,
and they're only a few steps behind you, finding
the flaw, the poor weld, the place where we weren't
stitched up quite right, the place they could almost
slip right through if the skin wasn't trying to
keep them out, to keep them here, on the other side
of the theater where the curtain keeps rising.
I crawled out the window and ran into the woods.

I had to make up all the words myself. The way
they taste, the way they sound in the air. I passed
through the narrow gate, stumbled in, stumbled
around for a while, and stumbled back out. I made
this place for you. A place for you to love me.
If this isn't the kingdom then I don't know what is.
So how would you catalog it? Dawn in the fields?
Snow and dirty rain? Light brought in in buckets?
I was trying to describe the kingdom, but the letters
kept smudging as I wrote them: the hunter's heart,
the hunter's mouth, the trees and the trees and the
space between the trees, swimming in gold. The words
frozen. The creatures frozen. The plum sauce
leaking out of the bag. Explaining will get us nowhere.
I was away, I don't know where, lying on the floor,
pretending I was dead. I wanted to hurt you
but the victory is that I could not stomach it. *We have
swallowed him up,* they said. *It's beautiful, it really is.*
I had a dream about you. We were in the gold room
where everyone finally gets what they want.
You said *Tell me about your books, your visions made
of flesh and light* and I said *This is the Moon. This is
the Sun. Let me name the stars for you. Let me take you
there. The splash of my tongue melting you like a sugar
cube* . . . We were in the gold room where everyone
finally gets what they want, so I said *What do you
want, sweetheart?* and you said *Kiss me.* Here I am
leaving you clues. I am singing now while Rome
burns. We are all just trying to be holy. My applejack,
my silent night, just mash your lips against me.
We are all going forward. None of us are going back.

Afterword

The manuscript was sloppy and I was afraid of it. I had adjusted it many times and sent it to contests every year for nine years. It was a glimmering failure. I sent it out again, feeling like this would probably be the last time I would try. When Louise Glück called, I was on the floor, unpacking boxes. I had just moved from a tiny apartment to a different tiny apartment with better windows. *I'm calling to let you know that I've selected your manuscript. We'll publish it as it is, of course, but I have notes if you'd like to consider them.* I was uncomfortable. Not because of the notes, but because it was Louise Glück. Of course I wanted the notes. *Good, because the manuscript is sloppy. It was not the best in the pile. I was reading manuscripts much better than yours, but while I was reading them I kept thinking about yours, so I knew it had to be the one.* I was no longer uncomfortable. This was someone I could work with.

I flew to Cambridge for the weekend. We were going to do a line edit at her kitchen table. I would stay at a B&B around the corner. I expected she would be severe and inscrutable. She expected I would be crazy and dangerous, with blood in my mouth. When she opened the door, I realized that she was the same size as my mom, with the same attitude. It turned out that she had a son the same size and age as me, also with a shaved head, also with wire-rimmed glasses. We knew what we were in for.

Yes, we argued. That Saturday we argued for twelve hours. We argued theory and aesthetics and history and intent. I read the poems out loud to her, in order, and she would stop me every time she had something to say, which was often. By the end of the day, we had cut a third of the book. We didn't cut poems, we cut sections. We cut gestures. We were bold. We cut things even if the poems had already been published. The manuscript had been sloppy because I was afraid of it. Every time I said something that scared me, I made a joke or swerved. She wasn't going to put up with it. Once I understood, I wasn't going to put up with it either. She had a keen eye, a perfect ear, and a mind that was diamond-sharp. I had ferocity, a deep commitment to language, and nothing to lose.

Louise was right about 90 percent of the time, and I got pretty good at anticipating her objections. I had internalized her concerns. I would read the lines and then stop to interrupt myself. The habit of turning away was systemic. But

10 percent of the time I was right. One line that I fought for, that I insisted wasn't silly—and I fought hard for it, for over an hour—is in the middle of "Saying Your Names." After a span of twenty-eight lines addressing the reader, the poem pivots and directly addresses the dead lover with a rising panic that isn't in the rest of the poem. It arrives at the line: "O now we're in the sea of love!" It has the only Romantic "O" in the poem. It has the only exclamation point in the poem. I think it's one of the saddest things I've ever written.

Did we cut too much? I don't think so. There's only one line I would put back in. I miss the version of "Visible World" that ended like this:

> The light is no mystery,
> the mystery is that there is something to keep the light
> from passing through.
> A river gone ice, so that we may walk across.

But cutting things left holes. And there were still glitches and awkward places where I hadn't taken the thought to the uncomfortable place it needed to go for the poem to be fully vulnerable and honest. Smoothing over those places would have made them polished but lifeless, so I would have to return to the moments and relive them, poke at them. Since there was nothing left to cut, we spent that Sunday afternoon in her garden, discussing generative strategies. "Boot Theory" had lost its ending. It was only after getting home and poking at it, over and over, that I found the ending it has now:

> A man takes his sadness down to the river and throws it in the river
> but then he's still left
> with the river. A man takes his sadness and throws it away
> but then he's still left with his hands.

There are several impulses that poets share when preparing our first books, and they all come from the same place: we feel like we are yelling into the void. We aren't used to being heard, not in this way, and there are so many things to say, so many approaches. It's hard to trust the reader. It's hard to write one book at a time when there's so much to say. We want to include everything—to say all of it, and all at the same time. We worry that this will be our only chance to say it. Instead of trusting the reader, I had filled the poems with blather and mud. *Not everyone is listening, but those that are are listening, are listening very closely.* Good advice. She also said—and maybe she was joking—*Be careful, every first book includes an Adam and Eve poem.* She was referring to "You Are Jeff." I was trying to address everything, including the book of Genesis. I cut more parts.

It was lean. Only the beautiful and necessary things remained. I wrote into it, trusting the reader, limiting my focus, speaking earnestly and with vulnerability. And then it was done. It went into the machinery and came out as a hardcover book. The box of my copies arrived in the mail. I waited for the applause, but nothing happened. Reviews did not appear; invitations to read did not arrive. Months passed. A year. Then, when the book started to get attention, the response surprised me. I didn't anticipate how many people would ask if it was a true story. *Did it really happen?* When I said it happened, they would pity me. When I said it didn't happen, they would call me a liar. I thought if I refused to answer, they would have to drop the questions about honesty and autobiography and confront the poems directly. I stopped answering. I refused to answer. It became a problem.

In fiction, we make the distinction between author and speaker. In poetry, we often conflate the two. The closeness between author and speaker in *Crush* made people curious. Perhaps the boldness of the poems made people bold with their questions. They wanted to know the story behind the story. It made me uncomfortable. I thought I had framed the poems in a variety of ways that would show they were acts of storytelling. I thought that the overlap and permutations of the characters in "You Are Jeff" would show the shifting nature of identity in the book. I had hoped that the use of the second person in the poems would complicate the speaker, make him multiple—that it would push the identity of the speaker onto the reader and make the reader complicit. *But did it really happen?* They would ask. They were confusing me with the work.

A high school student emailed me, saying, "My teacher is encouraging us to reach out to a living writer. I need to know 18 facts about your biography so I can understand your poems." I wrote back saying, basically, that if she needed my explanations and my biography to help her understand them—to feel them—then the poems were a failure and I had wasted my life. She wrote back, of course. She said I was rude and that now she was going to get a B. It made me mad. I, personally, was being interrogated rather than the work—and her questions had the undertone of "poetry isn't art" because her teacher refused to, or was unable to, understand that I had made a thing. They didn't see the thing; they only saw me. I started saying, *You get the page, I get the rest.* It went from motto to manifesto. Everything the reader needs is on the page. It has to be enough. Readers think they want more but really they don't. They don't need everything.

At the bank once, when the teller at the window recognized my name, she said, "I love the part where your boyfriend dies and you're really sad. How long were you together?" It seemed unfair. I wanted the freedom to keep some of my damages to myself so I could get through the day without being reminded of them. I wanted to make something that worked even when—especially when—I wasn't there. I liked not being there. I wanted the freedom to wander off, or fall asleep, and still have the poems work without me. And then someone wrote to say that they had used the poem "Scheherazade" at their wedding. And then someone else wrote that his girlfriend had hanged herself the night before and had left the poem "Scheherazade" as her suicide note. And then I got quiet. Having this book that *did this thing* had spooked me, and I felt a pressure to address it. But I didn't. I wouldn't.

It took ten years to get *Crush* published, and the world changed in the years between first draft and final manuscript. What I thought the work meant wasn't what the work meant anymore. What was originally a book about AIDS had arrived in a culture filled with vampires. The fear of blood had turned into fetish. The metaphors for blood were no longer focused on contamination and death. Instead, blood was now a conduit for romance, for eternal life. The light on everything had shifted. *Crush* had landed between cultural moments and it had two distinct audiences—one, still reeling from the impact of a devastating virus, the other informed by a culture that was embracing the *Twilight* movies and the TV shows *Supernatural* and *True Blood*. It was fascinating—no, terrifying—to hear what people thought the metaphors implied.

Other changes transformed the book as well. The first versions of the manuscript were printed on a Xerox machine. They were stapled in the corners. Now I have a website with links to all the poems—some in current magazines, some on people's abandoned blogs—and I don't have to pass around poems on paper in coffee shops. But the change in venue produced a change in form. It's hard to replicate line breaks and indentations online if you don't know HTML. And the size of a window changes dynamically, according to your settings, and that rebreaks the lines. The poems were getting greater exposure as people shared them, but people weren't seeing them in their original format. The poems were losing a significant part of their intent and their power.

The reason we break a line is to make a friction between the line and the sentence. We rub two units of meaning against each other. A break allows concurrent interpretations. It changes the emphasis. No other form of writing has this quality. A line break makes a hitch in the breath, a crack in the thought. There's a difference between *If you love me, Henry, you don't love me in a way I understand* and *If you love me, Henry, you don't love me / in a way I understand*. Line breaks make shapes, support voice, build architectures. I had an aesthetic, a philosophy, that was just as important to me as the content. It was disappearing. Most poetry is left-justified. We read a line and we come all the way back to baseline, then we read the next line and we come all the way back to baseline. The movement of the eye, always returning to the left, is predictable, almost exhausting. It feels like falling down, over and over. I wanted to sustain the momentum and defy gravity, so I indented lines. It was propulsive. The indentations kept the lines hovering in the air. Now they were gone.

Ten more years passed. We got camera phones and Photoshop. We got Facebook and Tumblr and Twitter. Fans were able to reproduce the poems as they appeared in the book, with the line breaks and indentations, but they were now pulling quotes out of context and putting them over pictures of cats or screenshots of their favorite shows. They returned the fidelity of the form to the text but they had abandoned its context. Fandoms embraced *Crush*, using lines as inspiration, or as text for memes, sometimes even interpolating large sections of the poems into their fan fiction. They championed remix culture and bristled at the idea that an author should be seen as the ultimate authority. People stopped asking me to confess or explain. It didn't matter to them what I thought the work meant or if things actually happened. They had their own ideas, and they were determined to explore them.

My twentieth-century intention had been to make a place where I could articulate my thoughts and feelings. I imagined that it would be a place where the reader and I could meet. That was no longer the way the poems were working. Readers were now enlarging the places I had made so they could include themselves. They were using this larger space to interact with each other without me. It was disconcerting. Some fans altered the male/male dynamic of the poems and posted their new, re-gendered versions. Some used the quotes in contexts that didn't make sense to me. Some misquoted the poems on purpose to suit their needs. I wanted readers to find meaning in the poems, even if that meaning slid away from my intention, but sometimes the revisions slid too far away from the original text. I felt as though my inner life was being translated into something unrecognizable.

It didn't help that the metaphors kept changing. *Crush* was moving between cultural moments again. Being gay in 2015 was different from being gay in 1995. It was still scary and dangerous but it wasn't unheard of; we weren't invisible anymore. The terror and loneliness of being gay that had informed the poems had diminished. The claustrophobic atmosphere of impending violence had been reframed. The violence was now being seen as a metaphor for personal transformation and not as a denunciation of the culture. The collisions and ruptures of self and other were now being seen as a type of communion. Only the confusion between speaker and author had remained the same. I had published another book by this time. I thought I was being crafty. Instead of talking about myself, I had written fables: I personified everything and played the ventriloquist. The fishsticks pondered and the moon spoke: the characters were animals or figures in paintings. It seemed like a foolproof plan to force a distinction between speaker and author. It didn't work. People still asked, "Is this true?" and it occurred to me that they were really asking, "Can this happen to me?" The answer to that was "Yes."

More years passed. The context kept changing. I wasn't sure which I would prefer: to have a book that was grounded in a moment of time or one that stayed restless and flexible. The idea of alternative facts started to percolate in the mind of the culture, and we swerved again. What good was metaphor in a post-truth world? What good is any of it if you can't trust the context or the source? Some poets turned to satire; others turned to nonfiction and activism. The lyric poets were singing into the voice-notes apps of their phones as they sequestered during the long COVID lockdowns. The quotes from *Crush* that were getting posted on Twitter were resonating with the dread and isolation of that moment. They were shimmering with it.

And still more years passed. We were creeping up on 2025. It seemed unreal. I had broken the spine on my only hardcover copy and I wanted a new one. I struck a deal with Yale University Press: they would produce a twentieth-anniversary edition of *Crush* if I would write an afterword. It was the opportunity to provide the backstage passes, to reclaim and recontextualize the work, to explain everything. I tried, at first. I did. But the work didn't belong to me, it never really belonged to me. It belonged to the reader. Similarly, the work wasn't about me either; it was about the reader. I can only comment on the changes I saw and how I felt about them. It sounds unfair until you realize that all the poems in the world that I didn't write belong to me, since I'm their audience.

What will happen over the next ten years? I can make some guesses. The most transgressive parts will become commonplace. The spotlight on the metaphors for vulnerability, violence, death will shift and illuminate new shades of meaning. Popular culture will introduce new examples of desire. (Vampires have already been replaced by cannibals—love as consumption—and the cannibals will soon be replaced by something else.) The context will continue to change as our focus changes. The interactions between reader and text will find new expressions. The language itself is changing. Having grown up texting, younger poets are currently reconsidering punctuation. Especially the period. It was too final, too absolute. They're abandoning it and turning to the line break and white space to make units of meaning. They read their work from phone screens. In my new book, I have abandoned the line and am trying to make the meaning happen in the space between the sentences. I'm using dictation software to write my poems instead of a notebook. What will remain the same? It's hard to say.

Once, at a reading, during the Q and A, someone in the audience asked what I thought about death. At first, I was put off—I wanted to talk about the poems—but these are the questions we expect poets to have the answers to. We expect poets to explore uncomfortable realms and return with secret knowledge. Sometimes we do. At the end of my second book, the speaker says, "I live in someone else's future." It's so obvious, it's terrifying. We document to share with the future. We benefit from the documents of the past. We say, *I was in this room once. It is a difficult room. I left this on the table for you. I hope it helps.* Whoever you are, reading this—it would have been nice to meet you, but I couldn't wait, I had to move on, I am already so far away.